# DISASTERS

# Hurricane ANDREW

Jen Green

GARETH**STEVENS**

GS

PUBLISHING
A WRC Media Company

**Please visit our web site at: www.garethstevens.com**
**For a free color catalog describing Gareth Stevens Publishing's list**
**of high-quality books and multimedia programs, call 1-800-542-2595 (USA)**
**or 1-800-387-3178 (Canada). Gareth Stevens Publishing's fax: (414) 332-3567.**

**Library of Congress Cataloging-in-Publication Data**

Green, Jen.
     Hurricane Andrew / Jen Green.
        p. cm. — (Disasters)
     Includes bibliographical references and index.
     ISBN 0-8368-4497-1 (lib. bdg.)
     1. Hurricane Andrew, 1992—Juvenile literature.  2. Hurricanes—
Juvenile literature.  I. Title.  II. Disasters (Milwaukee, Wis.)
     QC945.G63   2005
     363.34'922'09759—dc22                              2004056702

This edition first published in 2005 by
**Gareth Stevens Publishing**
A WRC Media Company
330 West Olive Street, Suite 100
Milwaukee, Wisconsin  53212  USA

Original copyright © 2004 The Brown Reference Group plc.  This U.S. edition
copyright © 2005 by Gareth Stevens, Inc.

Project Editor: Tim Cooke
Consultant: James A. Norwine, Professor of Geography, Texas A&M University
Designer: Lynne Ross
Picture Researcher: Becky Cox

Gareth Stevens series editor:  Jenette Donovan Guntly
Gareth Stevens art direction:  Tammy West

Picture credits: Front Cover: Corbis: Corbis Sygma.
Corbis: 17, Roger Ball 13, Bettmann 19, Corbis Sygma title page, 5, 23, Richard Gehman
12, 26, 27, Aaron Horowitz 2; Hulton-Deutsch 8, Reuters 10, Stocktrek 9; FEMA: 11, 25,
29; NASA:14; NOAA: 15, 18; Rex Features: 24; Topham: Larry Mulehill 21, Tony Savino 7.

Maps and Artwork: Brown Reference Group plc

Printed in the United States of America

1 2 3 4 5 6 7 8 9 09 08 07 06 05

**ABOUT THE AUTHOR**
Jen Green holds a doctorate in English and American studies. She has
been a children's author for over 20 years and has written more than
100 books for younger readers on many subjects, including history,
geography, and natural history. She lives in the south of England.

# CONTENTS

# 1 THE HURRICANE STRIKES

**In August 1992, Hurricane Andrew pounded the Caribbean and the southeastern United States. It was one of the fiercest hurricanes ever recorded in the United States and caused more damage than any other hurricane to hit that region.**

After causing damage to the Bahamas, which are islands in the Caribbean, Hurricane Andrew struck Florida's east coast on Monday, August 24, 1992. The towns of Homestead, Florida City, and Cutler Ridge near Miami got hit the worst. Andrew raged on across the tip of Florida. It crossed the Gulf of Mexico and struck south-central Louisiana, where it caused more damage. A hurricane is a huge, spinning storm in which winds reach speeds of 74 miles (119 kilometers) per hour or more. In all, Andrew killed more than sixty people. It caused more than $25 billion in damage in Florida and $1 billion in Louisiana. It was the most expensive natural disaster in U.S. history.

### BIRTH OF THE STORM

Hurricane Andrew was the first major storm of 1992. During the warm, summer months, violent, spinning storms build up over **tropical** oceans. Andrew came to life as thunderstorms

▼ Strong winds pound a street in Miami, Florida, in August 1992. The worst-hit places were Miami and other communities in Dade County.

UNITED STATES OF AMERICA

KANSAS · MISSOURI · KENTUCKY · VIRGINIA · N. CAROLINA · TENNESSEE · S. CAROLINA · OKLAHOMA · ARKANSAS · ALABAMA · GEORGIA · MISSISSIPPI · TEXAS · LOUISIANA · Galveston

**Florida**

· Kissimmee
· Fort Lauderdale
· Miami
· Homestead
Florida Keys

**Atlantic Ocean**

**Gulf of Mexico**

**Bahamas**

**Cuba**

## RATING HURRICANE ANDREW

Hurricane Andrew rates as the third most powerful hurricane to hit the United States. The two most powerful hurricanes were a hurricane that struck the Florida Keys on Labor Day in 1935 and Hurricane Camille, which battered the southeastern United States in 1969. When Andrew struck Florida's east coast, the National Hurricane Center in southern Miami measured steady winds of 145 miles (233 km) per hour. One wind gust reached 177 miles (285 km) per hour. These wind speeds placed Andrew in category 4 on the Saffir–Simpson Hurricane Scale, which is the standard scale scientists use to rate hurricanes. Both the Labor Day Hurricane and Camille scored a category 5, the highest rating. Andrew's rating was later increased to category 5 (see box on page 24).

▲ The red line on this map shows the route of Hurricane Andrew through the Bahamas, across the southern tip of Florida, and then into Louisiana. By the time the storm headed northeast from Louisiana, it had lost most of its power.

◄ Floridians board up windows and doors before the hurricane strikes. It is important to board up all openings to try to prevent strong winds from blowing into buildings and causing lots of damage.

near West Africa on August 13. After Andrew moved west, out over the Atlantic Ocean, it gained strength. Andrew became a hurricane spinning around an eye, which is a column of still air in the middle of the hurricane.

Late on August 21, Andrew turned west toward Florida. Radio and television stations put out hurricane warnings, and more than a million residents got into their cars and fled. Other people settled down to endure the storm as best they could.

## IN THE HURRICANE'S PATH

On Sunday, August 23, 1992, the storm struck the Bahamas with winds of up to 155 miles (250 km) per hour. It wrecked towns and

## FACT FILE

WHERE: Bahamas, southern Florida, central Louisiana

WHEN: August 23 to August 26, 1992

TOTAL TIME: About 144 hours

SPEED: 165 mile (265 km) per hour winds, with wind gusts of up to 200 miles (322 km) per hour

COSTS: $26 billion in United States

KILLED OR INJURED: More than sixty dead

# EYEWITNESS

*"I will always remember the sound. You know how a trumpet squeals when the player is really straining? That was the sound at the front door. The wood was buckling and through that seam between the double doors the wind was screaming to get through. The noise was incredible. You couldn't really hear individual things smashing because of the overall roar. It was that freight train you always hear described. Like it was running right through the house."*

*– Ben Horenstein*

# HURRICANES IN HISTORY

The southeastern region of the United States has a long history of hurricanes. During the first half of the twentieth century, many strong hurricanes struck the area. Very strong storms in the 1920s and 1930s included the 1935 Labor Day Hurricane, which destroyed much of the Florida Keys. Between 1940 and 1950, no fewer than five major hurricanes raised **storm surges** that flooded areas along the coast. Hurricane Donna pounded the Florida Keys in the 1960s, followed by Cleo and, in 1965, Betsy, which was a category 3 hurricane. After the mid-1960s, however, no major tropical storms had struck Florida's east coast—until the fateful morning of August 24, 1992.

▶ **Residents inspect damaged apartments in downtown Miami after the 1935 Labor Day Hurricane that hit southern Florida.**

farmland, and killed four people. Early Monday morning, Andrew whirled across Florida's Biscayne Bay to strike Miami-Dade County.

The whirling winds whipped up a 17-foot (5-meter) storm surge. The sea flooded coastal vacation resorts. It carried boats inland. Winds howling at 165 miles (265 km) per hour pulled windows, roofs, and walls off of apartment and office buildings. Trees were uprooted and became deadly missiles flying through the air. At the U.S. Air Force base at Homestead, the hurricane tossed planes around like toys.

Andrew's funnel of high winds moved across the southern tip of Florida at about

▲ **This dramatic image taken from a satellite shows the movement of Hurricane Andrew as it passes over the Bahamas (right), Florida (center), and Louisiana (left).**

9

18 miles (29 km) per hour. It ripped through orchards and flattened fields. In the swamps of the Everglades in Florida, it stripped leaves off trees. The storm surrounded the entire **peninsula**. The fiercest winds gusted at up to 200 miles (320 km) per hour in a small area around the eye. The hurricane left a path of destruction some 25 miles (40 km) wide and 60 miles (96 km) long.

As Andrew whirled on, Floridians inspected the damage. About eighty thousand homes were wrecked and fifty-five thousand homes

▲ **A Dade County resident looks up at a passing helicopter after the storm passed. Hurricane Andrew's winds tore roofs off many buildings and knocked down walls.**

# REPORTING THE DISASTER

Television weatherman Bryan Norcross of Miami's WTVJ station became a local hero for his news stories about Hurricane Andrew. For a long time, he had feared that a violent tropical storm would hit southern Florida. After carefully following Andrew's path across the Atlantic Ocean, Norcross told viewers to prepare for the "big one." On the evening of Sunday, August 23, 1992, he warned, "It's absolutely for sure. No question about it. It's going to happen tonight." Norcross kept broadcasting on the television as the storm hit. He gave advice and comforted his viewers. In contrast, some national news groups were too slow in understanding how big the storm would become. Instead of reporting the story in Florida, many of their reporters moved on to Louisiana to follow Andrew's progress.

► **This truck was blown over by the hurricane. The high winds also snapped poles carrying power cables.**

were badly damaged. Trailer parks were destroyed. The storm left 1.4 million people without power or water and many without food. In nine-year-old Kristen Benitez's house in Homestead, Florida, "The winds were so strong they cleared out all of the cabinets." Her family had no food for two days.

After the disaster, hungry people stole food and drinks from wrecked stores and homes. People also began to loot, or steal, valuable items such as televisions and computers. Some residents pointed guns at the looters and made them return the things they had taken.

Hundreds of dogs and cats were left behind and roamed southern Miami. Animals from

**▼ A volunteer veterinarian cleans a wound to a dog's head. Many pet owners left their animals behind when they fled the storm. Other pets were injured by flying debris or were thrown around in the wind.**

▶ After Hurricane Andrew, only a few trailers were left standing in this trailer park near Kissimmee, Florida. The hurricane wrecked many trailers, because they were not strong enough to hold together in the powerful winds.

## EYEWITNESS

*"There were no windows left in any of the cars. Trees, fences, light poles were all over the roads. When we made it back to our rented house, the roof was gone. A tree had fallen on the car we left there. Everything inside was soaked and covered with fiberglass from the insulation. It was all ruined."*

*– Cristen Oliver*

destroyed farms wandered the countryside. Experts even caught a python and a cougar that had escaped from a zoo.

### THE END OF ANDREW

While people tried to recover in Florida, Hurricane Andrew swept across the Gulf of Mexico. It struck the coast of south-central Louisiana early on Wednesday, August 26, 1992. Winds roared at up to 120 miles (190 km) per hour. An 8-foot (2.5-m) storm surge pounded towns along the coast. Andrew tore through **marshlands**, sugarcane fields, and towns. As it turned northeast, it lost strength. The storm finally died down and became a series of **squalls** that struck the southeastern United States on August 27 and 28.

# 2 WHAT ARE HURRICANES?

**Hurricane Andrew was the third most powerful hurricane ever to strike the United States. Hurricanes and other strong tropical storms cause lots of damage in countries around the world.**

When seen from above, hurricanes look like giant pinwheels. They have bands of cloud spinning around a central "eye." Hurricanes begin as thunderstorms that gather over tropical oceans during hot and **humid** weather.

Hurricanes only form over oceans where the water is warmer than 78 degrees Fahrenheit (26 degrees Celsius). They often form in the Atlantic Ocean just north of the **equator**. Most hurricanes then move west toward the Caribbean and the eastern coasts of the Americas. Few hurricanes form in the South Atlantic, which is colder.

In the Indian Ocean, hurricanes often strike nations in South Asia.

▼ **This satellite image shows Andrew as a white swirl hitting the coast of Louisiana (boxed area in upper right of picture).**

► **This image from a satellite shows (in dark blues and blacks) the heavy buildup of water vapor in Andrew as it swirls through the islands of the Caribbean.**

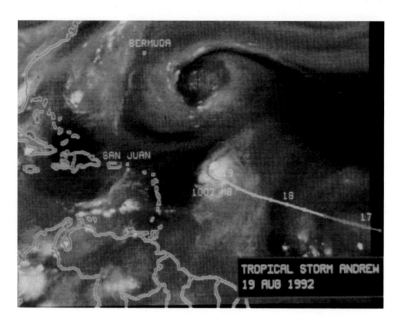

Hurricanes in the Indian Ocean are called tropical cyclones. Hurricanes in the Pacific Ocean, which are called typhoons, threaten Japan, the islands of Indonesia, and Australia.

When a storm is large enough to be called a **tropical storm**, it is given a name. The first name given each year starts with A, such as Andrew. The next storm's name starts with B, and so on. In the past, all tropical storms and hurricanes had female names. Now, a female name is given, then a male name, and so forth.

### HOW DO HURRICANES FORM?

A hurricane starts to form as heat from the Sun **evaporates** moisture from the sea. The warm, damp air rises. Cooler air rushes in to replace it, creating winds. Earth's spin causes the winds to turn and spiral inward.

15

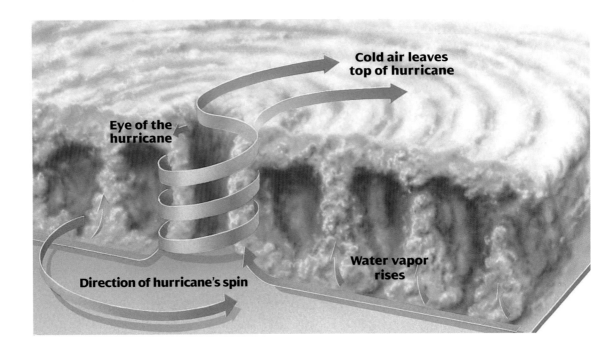

Cold air leaves
top of hurricane

Eye of the
hurricane

Water vapor
rises

Direction of hurricane's spin

▲ This drawing of the inside of a hurricane shows how water vapor (red arrows) rises and adds to a storm. The water vapor cools as it rises through the eye of the hurricane. As it cools, the water vapor is shed as rain. Cool air then spins out of the top of the hurricane (blue arrows). The cool air flows against the direction in which the hurricane is spinning (bottom red arrow).

As the warm air rises, water vapor in the air **condenses** to form drops of water that become thunderclouds. The clouds shed huge amounts of rain. The condensing of the water also releases heat, making the winds stronger and stronger. The storm spreads as it draws air in at its base. The air spirals around the central eye, which is the main feature of a hurricane. The strongest winds are in the tight funnel of dark clouds spinning directly around the eye.

As the hurricane sweeps across the ocean at speeds of up to 30 miles (50 km) per hour, it whips up towering waves. The waves spread outward and sometimes reach coasts days before the hurricane itself arrives. The waves are formed when the ocean surface is sucked upward by the **low pressure** at the heart of

# THE WORLD'S WORST HURRICANES

▼ **This airplane was flipped onto a roof in the Dominican Republic by Hurricane David in 1979. David killed four thousand people.**

Many different parts of the world have been struck by powerful hurricanes in the last fifty years or so. In 1959, terrible flooding caused by Typhoon Vera killed more than 5,000 people in Japan. In 1970, a cyclone hit the country of Bangladesh in Asia, killing 500,000 people. It was one of the world's worst natural disasters. Another powerful cyclone killed 250,000 people in that same region in 1991. In 1974, 8,000 people died when Hurricane Fifi struck Honduras in Central America. In 1979, Hurricane David killed 4,000 people when it hit Puerto Rico, the Dominican Republic, and the southeastern United States. Compared to these disasters, Hurricane Andrew killed many fewer people, despite its great strength.

the storm. A huge mound of water builds up under the eye. When this mound of water flows out and strikes land, it causes a storm surge. Hurricane Andrew's storm surge flooded Florida's east coast on August 24, 1992. In 1900, a storm surge caused the deadliest natural disaster in U.S. history. A hurricane struck the port of Galveston, which stands on a low-lying island just off the coast of Texas.

The high seas washed over the island, causing large amounts of damage and drowning about eight thousand people.

A hurricane's strength comes from the flow of warm, damp air that continues to rise up from the ocean. As the storm sweeps across tropical oceans, it is kept going by the water vapor that is added along the way. Hurricanes usually begin to die down as they reach land, where the supply of warm, damp air is cut off.

Some hurricanes go against this general rule, however. Experts believe that Hurricane Andrew got stronger for a short time after striking land in the United States. No one is quite sure why this happened.

▲ **People wade through a flooded street in Galveston, Texas, in September 1900. The Galveston Hurricane killed more than eight thousand people—more than any other disaster in U.S. history.**

Today, experts know that a hurricane's strongest winds are small vortexes. Vortexes are funnels of air that spiral inside the wall of clouds around the hurricane's eye. Thousands of vortexes formed and then broke apart inside Andrew as it made its way across Florida. The vortexes left tell-tale trails of worse damage where they traveled than in the wider area of damage caused by the whole hurricane.

### HURRICANE SCIENCE

No one can control the terrible power of a hurricane. However, scientists have learned a lot about the natural forces that create and

▶ People have piled their belongings on the roofs of their homes, which were flooded by Hurricane Fifi in Honduras in 1974. Along with high winds, floods are one of the most damaging parts of a hurricane.

# TORNADOES

Hurricanes are sometimes confused with tornadoes because both are types of violent, spinning storms that can cause great damage. The two weather events happen on an entirely different scale, however. Hurricanes are huge spinning storms that can measure up to 1,250 miles (2,000 km) wide. Tornadoes are far smaller. They are often only about one-half mile (1 km) across. Hurricanes often rage for days and sometimes even weeks. Most tornadoes last only minutes, even though they do large amounts of damage. Another difference is that tornadoes form on land, while hurricanes are formed far out at sea.

▼ A tornado swirls through a cornfield in the Midwest in 2001.

feed these tropical storms. In 1959, the National Hurricane Center was created to study every part of a hurricane. At the center, scientists called meteorologists, who study weather, look at the buildup of energy within hurricanes and where a hurricane's energy is the strongest.

The meteorologists use various methods to gather facts. Since the 1960s, they have used satellites. Cameras and other equipment on

▶ **Two meteorologists study information at the U.S. National Hurricane Center in Miami, Florida. The center was set up in 1959 to study hurricanes and provide warnings of storms before they arrive.**

satellites circling Earth produce lots of useful information about storms. They make it much easier to spot a hurricane forming and to track its course across the oceans. Another way to gather information about hurricanes is by flying aircraft as near to them as possible. The aircraft have tools to measure wind speed and direction, air temperature, and air pressure.

Information from satellites, aircraft, and weather stations around the world is fed into supercomputers. The computers chart a hurricane's path and where it is likely to head. The predictions are constantly checked and changed. This allows officials to give correct hurricane warnings well in advance. Areas that are in danger can prepare for the storm or people can move out of the hurricane's way.

# 3 THE AFTERMATH OF THE DISASTER

**The cleanup in Florida and Louisiana started just hours after Hurricane Andrew passed. The storm had a lasting effect, both on the area and on plans in case of another disaster.**

In the worst-hit parts of Florida and Louisiana, power lines were down, traffic filled the roads, and people ran out of food and clean water. The officials were slow to realize the full scale of the disaster. At first, there was little help for Andrew's victims.

After two days, Kate Hall, who was director of emergency management in Dade County, Florida, held a meeting for reporters. She said, "We need food. We need water. We need people." Her plea for help brought results. Sixteen thousand National Guard and army troops arrived, along with the Red Cross and other emergency groups, including the Federal Emergency Management Agency (FEMA). The soldiers stopped the looting, cleared debris, and set up camps for the homeless. Food, clothing, and other supplies began to arrive.

Volunteers, many from other parts of the country, came to south Florida to help. Many people felt bad for the victims of Hurricane

▶ Workers repair telephone lines in Homestead, Florida, two weeks after Hurricane Andrew. The storm wrecked the town and brought down many power and telephone lines in the region.

## UPGRADING ANDREW

Hurricane science is being updated all the time. Since 1992, when Hurricane Andrew hit, new equipment has made it possible to better keep track of tropical storms. Since 1997, instruments called Global Positioning System (GPS) dropwindsondes have been dropped into hurricanes from aircraft. The dropwindsondes take measurements inside storms as they drift down through hurricanes on parachutes. Information from these new machines has made scientists rethink their measurements of wind speeds inside hurricanes. As a result, they have decided that Andrew was more powerful than they thought. They have upgraded Andrew to a category 5 hurricane. It is now considered just as powerful as the 1935 Labor Day Hurricane and Hurricane Camille in 1969.

▼ **This sign was put up by residents to stop looting. When the National Guard got to Florida, stopping the looting was one of their first tasks.**

Andrew. One person said, "It's made a lot of people realize . . . all them things they worked years for could be took from 'em real fast. Now we got to learn to stick together."

### EFFECTS OF THE STORM

Today, more than ten years after Hurricane Andrew, southern Florida and Louisiana have mostly recovered. Some scars still remain, however. About six hundred thousand homes and businesses were wrecked or badly damaged, along with half a million boats and the air force base at Homestead. Most of the damage was caused by high winds and some by storm surges and heavy rain.

In all, more than sixty people died in the storm. Storm warnings saved many more lives, however. During the storm, more than one million people fled south Florida. About one hundred thousand people left Dade County for good. Some people could afford to move out of the area, but others could not and were forced to stay. The region's economy has been slow to recover. Today, most Dade County residents do not have good jobs and many people are poor.

▼ **This Federal Emergency Management Agency (FEMA) camp was set up in Florida to house people left homeless by the storm.**

▲ Floridians sort through groceries at a center set up to give out food after the storm. Many people were left with no food at all after the hurricane.

Hurricane Andrew was the most expensive natural disaster in U.S. history. It could have been worse, however. If the storm had turned northeast as it struck land, as experts thought it might, it would have hit the crowded areas of downtown Miami and Fort Lauderdale. Many more people could have died. Rainfall was also light, so rivers did not flood. Andrew's worst damage happened in an area that was no more than 40 miles (65 km) wide. Moving at 18 miles (29 km) per hour, the storm also passed over somewhat quickly, which lessened the damage.

Damage to the region's wildlife and plants could also have been worse. Hurricane Andrew destroyed about one-third of the coral reefs in Florida's Biscayne National Park. More than 9 million fish also died when they could not breathe in water filled with oil from damaged boats. Coral reefs in the Florida Keys were not hurt, however. About 700,000 acres (280,000 hectares) of Florida's mangrove swamps were badly damaged, but the freshwater **wetlands** of the Everglades suffered little damage.

Overall, most wildlife was able to survive the storm, but in Louisiana, millions of fish died. They could not breathe when the storm stirred up mud in rivers and lakes, which cut the amount of oxygen in the water. Forests in

▼ **A great blue heron perches on a pine tree that was snapped in half by Hurricane Andrew. Despite the damage caused by the storm, the wildlife and plants of Florida and Louisiana were able to recover somewhat quickly.**

## THE 2004 HURRICANE SEASON

In 2004, the hurricane season, which lasts from the beginning of June to the end of November, was the worst season in the past one hundred years. Before the season was even over, four major storms pounded Florida. Hurricane Charley hit in August and was followed in September by hurricanes Frances, Ivan, and Jeanne.

Lessons from Hurricane Andrew helped Floridians better deal with the 2004 hurricanes. Officials warned more than 2.5 million people to move out of the danger area, so fewer people died. All four storms together killed about the same number of people that Andrew killed alone. Also, new, stronger buildings were able to withstand the winds, so there was less damage. Damage from all four storms cost less than the $26 billion that Andrew cost.

the state also suffered serious damage, but new growth began to sprout from the damaged trees in less than a month.

### RECOVERY AND LESSONS LEARNED

Hurricane Andrew changed how Americans prepare for natural disasters. Many people said officials reacted too slowly to the disaster. New guidelines that outline how to respond to hurricanes will make sure that state, federal, and local groups work together in the event of another large disaster.

The hurricane also showed that many homes were not safe. Trailer parks suffered very badly. Some experts say that the parks should be against the law in areas where hurricanes often hit. The storm also showed how sloppily some buildings were put together. High winds broke through weak doors or windows and then blew off roofs from inside.

Florida now has tough new building codes. They are the toughest in the nation. All new buildings must have strong shutters on the doors and windows and very strong roofs. Homestead and other towns wrecked by Andrew have been rebuilt. They have stronger houses and new public centers. When four storms nearly as large as Hurricane Andrew pounded Florida in 2004, the state was in much better shape to survive them.

▼ A crane tears down a home damaged by Hurricane Andrew. Many buildings had weak windows and doors that let in the wind, which could then blow off roofs and knock down walls.

# GLOSSARY

**condenses** Changes from a gas to a liquid or solid. When water in warm, damp air cools, it collects to become droplets, such as rain.

**debris** Pieces left when something has been broken up or destroyed.

**equator** An imaginary line running east to west around the middle of Earth, dividing it into two halves.

**evaporates** Turns from a liquid into a vapor or gas when heated.

**humid** related to very damp air.

**low pressure** An area of warm air. It weighs less than cool air and puts less pressure on the ground. The warm air rises and cools and often sheds moisture as storms.

**marshlands** Areas of land that are always soft and damp. Usually, tall plants such as grasses grow there.

**peninsula** A long, thin piece of land that has water surrounding it on three sides.

**satellite** A machine put into space to circle the Earth. A satellite can carry radio and television signals or can photograph and measure the weather on Earth.

**squalls** Short, sudden windstorms that often carry rain or snow.

**storm surges** Large waves that have been created by winds from storms far out to sea.

**tropical** related to warm and wet regions located near the equator.

**tropical storm** A spinning storm with wind speeds from 39 to 73 miles (63 to 118 km) per hour.

**veterinarian** A doctor trained to take care of sick or hurt animals.

**water vapor** Water in the form of a gas. It is created when water is heated. It collects to form clouds.

**wetlands** Areas of land where the soil is always wet, including near waterways that often overflow.

# FURTHER RESEARCH

## BOOKS

Challoner, Jack. *Hurricane and Tornado (Eyewitness Books)*. NY: Dorling Kindersley, 2004.

Lauber, Patricia. *Hurricanes: Earth's Mightiest Storms*. NY: Scholastic, 1996.

Murray, Peter. *Hurricanes (Forces of Nature* series). Chanhassen, MN: Child's World, 1999.

Sherrow, Victoria. *Hurricane Andrew: Nature's Rage (American Disasters* series). Springfield, NJ: Enslow Publishers, 1998.

Spilsbury, Louise, and Richard Spilsbury. *Howling Hurricanes (Awesome Forces of Nature* series). Chicago: Heinemann Library, 2004.

## WEB SITES

*Cyberflight: Hurricane Hunters*
www.hurricanehunters.com

*Flying into the Eye of a Hurricane: National Geographic Kids*
www.nationalgeographic.com/ngkids/0308/hurricane/

*Hurricane: Storm Science, Miami Museum of Science*
www.miamisci.org/hurricane

*Hurricanes: Enchanted Learning*
www.enchantedlearning.com/subjects/weather/hurricane/

*Hurricanes: Federal Emergency Management Agency (FEMA)*
www.fema.gov/kids/hurr.htm

*Hurricanes: Kidstorm, Sky Diary*
skydiary.com/kids/hurricanes.html

# INDEX